Live, Love, Paws

Your Guide to Living Long and Loving Deeply

Dr. Jen Furcht and Dr. Jamie Sarra

Copyright © 2016 by Dr. Jen Furcht
All rights reserved. No part of this book may be reproduced, scanned, or distributed in any printed or electronic form without permission.
Second Edition: March 2019

In memory of Captain
For all the people who want to live inspired,
For those who have been touched by their pet,

Printed in the United States of America
ISBN: 978-0999426524

TABLE OF CONTENTS

Table of Contents i
Dedication ii
Preface 1
Presence 4
Grounding 6
Purpose 8
Patience 10
Simplicity 12
Vulnerability 14
Forgiveness 16
Movement 18
Soul Food 20
Personal Power 22
Healing 24
Communication 26
Kindness 29
Joy 30
Gratitude 32
Aging 34
Willingness 36
Miracles 38
Trust 40
Grace 42
See The Signs 44
Unconditional Love 46

DEDICATION

We would like to dedicate this book to all Beings. May you step in these pawprints and walk the lessons in your own life, and see the gifts that are brought forth through your own animals and the loved ones surrounding you.

We would like to thank Captain for bringing these lessons forward and for expanding our hearts. You have opened your family up to a new way of living because of the unconditional love you shared and continue to share everyday.

Captain would like to dedicate this book of Life Lessons to his Moms, family and friends who loved and supported him through his many stages of life. He would also like to extend these teachings to all people who love their animals and have experienced the loss of their beloved friend and companion.

In honor of Captain and all rescue animals, for every book sold a donation will be made to support the animal rescues.

PREFACE

Dr. Jen Furcht

Animals are amazing and have a way of Being that holds the secrets of how to live a life of love and abundance. This book is a soulful message, intuitively written through the eyes of Captain, my dog and companion. It's intention is simply to make your life better.

As a bioenergetic doctor and empowerment consultant, I am fortunate to be a teacher in the art of universal law, healing, and energy work. I've had the opportunity to interact with phenomenal people with unique stories of tragedy and hope.

With this life path in mind, I visited many places around the world, answering some of my questions as to why we are here and what the big picture is.

Every person has to move through loss. The moment the shift occurs in life there is much to process. When physical loss happens, it can feel like you forget everything you have learned and felt to be true in your world. When I was in that space, I remembered to go back to my own teachings that I had advised to others during their times of challenge. In stillness, Captain began to come alive through my pen and heart. I started to feel all the things he taught me: twenty-two teachings of our time together.

Captain acted as a connector. What I realized is that he set a stage to notice fully, the consistent love I had from my parents, sister, and family. In addition, he helped me experience love within myself, so I could be available and unconditionally open to finding love with my partner Jamie. She came along and brought us all to a new level of joy I didn't know life could hold. In my heart, I thank Captain for these gifts. Captain made a dent in the universe, and we hope that he also makes an imprint in your life as well.

In love and blessings,

Dr. Jen Furcht and Dr. Jamie Sarra

Lesson 1
PRESENCE

The first lesson in life begins with knowing presence. To be your best self, you must first center and feel the flow of nature. To be here fully, feel the love, and make good decisions, we must breathe into the body and wake up from the inside out. This means you wake up and say, "I am ready for this life experience"–that I am ready to play, chase sticks, connect with my family, and live in joy.

Presence is more than simply focusing on the experience. Presence is knowing that the deeper you can connect with yourself, the more you open up doors to infinite possibilities. When present, know you have the power to be the ultimate creator in your life. When you feel this energy, you can direct your attention and intention to make a shift. Make every breath count and experience it all.

Lesson 2

GROUNDING

When you come home from a stressful day, part of my job as a healer is to ground you. I show up at the door with joy to help you shift your energy back to its natural state. If you are not attending to your thoughts, actions, and feelings in a positive way, as the healer, I take this on for you.

I am here for you always, but this is also your training to be a master in your own universe. I teach you how to do this by going for walks, being in silence, connecting with the ocean, and planting myself in the grass. Want to put your paws in the Earth? Become one with the Earth. Feel yourself rooted to the central core, as roots extend downward, out of your own feet. Feel the support from the Earth.

I do this naturally, and I am doing this for you all the time. Through what is going on with me, I am constantly showing you what is out of balance in your life. If you love yourself, and me, you will attend to your energy in how you are Being. This way, I don't have to always take on the stress, and

---

Visit www.DrJenFurcht.com/breath

For a breath that enhances presence, relaxes your system, & allows energy to flow in your life.

therefore, I can also Be at peace. With this connection, your body has the opportunity to heal. You have to Be present in your body for it to work optimally. Grounding and healing is your daily responsibility. It will bring us both health and ease, and eventually when my physical presence is gone, the training wheels come off, and it is up to you.

"Paws," and take a breath

1. Plant yourself in the grass or envision nature
2. Feel roots extend from your feet down into the central core of the Earth
3. Breathe into your belly–exhale into the Earth–feel the support
4. Inhale from the Earth back into your belly
5. Feel the energy expand

Ahhhh. Doesn't that feel better?

Lesson 3
PURPOSE

What is your purpose? In your life you will be searching for what it is you are supposed to be doing here. The truth is that you are already the purpose. Purpose is the essence of who you are and the joy of us being together and experiencing life. All I do for you and me is my purpose, every moment and every breath. When I lead with this, amazing things unfold. My life flows in a stream of peace. I create all that I could ever imagine without even needing to know what is to come next. Relax and find presence. Watch how it all comes together. It will be beyond what you could have ever imagined. This is the secret, and you can lean on me always.

Whatever you are doing, laying in your favorite space, going for a joy ride, eating a steak, or loving your favorite humans, you fulfill purpose. You can't not fulfill purpose when it comes from LOVE; even the seemingly small things invite pure purpose. Purpose is an act of presence. There is nothing to do; you are already IT. All you seek will find you.

Lesson 4

PATIENCE

In any moment, especially the tough ones, take your time, move to a quiet space, and know eventually someone will come to pet you. It is in this practice that you come to trust yourself and the world. Patience allows time to stand still. You sit and stay, even when you think you should move forward.

In the stillness, you begin to know that everything will work out, and you don't always have to go after the treats—they actually come to you. I learned patience because I trusted you would always come home to me and love me. In return, I am always waiting at home for you and extending my love. It is the infinite flow that allows the joy of this reward. Just know, you are never alone because we are all one. Patience is trusting—it is safe to just Be.

Lesson 5
SIMPLICITY

What if life were simple? What if humans are the ones who create the limiting ideas? *Healing is a process; finances are a struggle; people are bad; the world is not fair; things shouldn't happen the way they do*....then, we wonder why freedom becomes blocked. Why complicate existence?

What if the truth is, we are the creators, and the universe is supporting our every move...that in every moment, you understood how truly powerful you are, orchestrating it all. How would you live?

One of the great things about being a dog is that in my world, we don't engage in the drama. We keep it simple, which is as close to the truth as you can get. It is what it is; without the interpretation of what could, would, or should be. We are the models for knowing how to just Be in the moment. We have the ability to flow with nature and appreciate life. We don't take situations and add perceived scenarios, drawing from the past, trying to connect unnecessary dots in life experiences. Remember anything that is not simple is not the truth. The more we try and figure it all out, the more we move away from the stillness where the answers reside. There is a force within us that always knows; this is the true you beyond the made up facts and figures.

If it is not simple, move on. Energy is everything, and if it is not moving, then there will be complication, unhappiness, and stress. We are here to teach a way of freedom in life. You are each unique in your own way, and to express this fully, simplicity will guide you to feel understood, be seen, and have your message heard.

Lesson 6
Vulnerability

Even when you have experienced hurt before by another human, or have felt abandoned in life, be open to the idea of dropping your guards. Lay on your back, open your heart, enjoy the clouds in the sky, and let someone get close again. In this, we find our true companions, and we rescue each other. The purpose is to continue to love no matter what, and the belly rub is worth it.

Life is ever changing. Something you see as true today may not be true tomorrow. To be vulnerable and open to change, we have to do what we have not done before. We must be flexible in mind and body and feel safe enough to recognize outdated habits and belief systems. These negative beliefs hold us back and prevent us from being close with others, letting in love, and moving forward in life. Instead of doing things based on what I've done in the past, I do things from an authentic view and become the master of my own self-action. I am open to vulnerability and positive change. The constant is the love underneath it all. Focus on that, allow and watch the waterfall of love exist.

Lesson 7
FORGIVENESS

When you come into the house and see that I have done wrong, look at my cute face and forgive me, as I always forgive you. Forgive yourself for being home later than you expected. Learn the lesson in the moment. Love is stronger, and our bond is more important. Remember though, this is easy to do with me, because I am the definition of unconditional love. Bring this love out into the world with all you see going on around you.

Forgiveness is about you and your health. The transformation comes from the ability to forgive yourself and another as you connect with your inner teacher. You have a choice to create love or fear, health or dis-ease. How do you want your energy to continue to vibrate? Your well-being is reflected in the ability to feel the energy and then let go and forgive. Your experience is the way it is supposed to be for your expansion…

…and yes, even that!

Because you're a human, let me lay this out for you:

1. Forgive Yourself
2. Forgive Another
3. Allow yourself to feel what you are feeling
4. Engage with the feeling and breathe it through your body
5. See the lesson
6. Let Go

Lesson 8
MOVEMENT

Living by this lesson, I lived to be a fifteen year old pup. I stayed young and healthy for over a 100 human years. I stretch and play everyday. I follow my breath while stretching. Some call it yoga. I call it the BooBoo downward dog. Your mind slows down when you do this. Following your breath keeps you present and feeling powerful. It activates your inner self. Start your day here and notice peace. You are life force. As this force moves more freely, you can feel the love, the true you. This is where vitality resides.

Are you consciously choosing a healthful exercise? Some exercise breaks you down, while others build you up. It can depend on your stage in life as well as your quality of current health. Your needs can change daily. Exercise is about healthy flow and doing every movement with consciousness. To do any activity for optimal benefits, you must engage at and move from your core, which is your powerhouse. I do this well and therefore was able to maintain fluid joints, a healthy blood system, and astute mental clarity.

Exercise alone will not get you here. It is all about bringing the energy in, engaging and balancing your body. Everyday, I wake up, take a deep breath, elongate my spine, and stretch out my paws. I do this naturally. Do you? If you keep this in mind your body will respond and reflect a strong vessel for your life experience. Your body is your temple and is a place for your spirit to reside. You feel more of your spirit with conscious movement. Intend to notice that you are self-healing and can accomplish anything you want. Your body is a miracle!

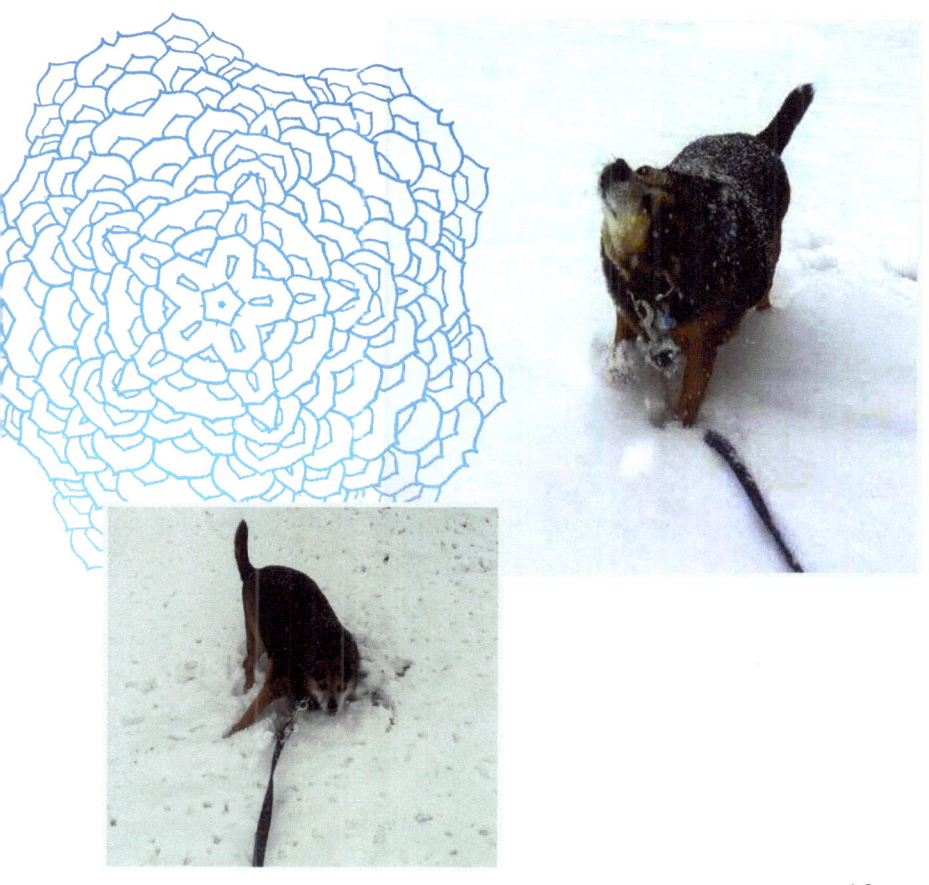

Lesson 9
SOUL FOOD

One of my favorite parts of the day, other than going for a ride, or taking walks with my family, my pack, was eating. Every day I would wake up to the squeak of the pantry door opening or a bag crinkling—my ears would rise, and my nose would twitch like a bunny. I would wait to see what treat was coming my way. My day would start by getting one of my favorites: coconut oil on a spoon. I loved the taste. It kept my coat shiny, my heart in check, and my joints pain free. In the late afternoon, I would wait patiently in the kitchen for the oven timer to ding. My mom would home cook all natural foods for me. These foods allowed my body to heal, so I could live happy.

I had a hard time eating processed foods. I always had a sense that I needed whole healthy nutrition like free-range chicken, wild salmon, grass-fed beef, organic wild rice, sprouted sunflower seeds, fresh organic apples, and carrots. I knew these foods would feed my body and bring my whole being to a state of purity and fullness. I wouldn't eat anything else because I knew it would cut my life short.

Aside from the physical nourishment, my moms nourished my soul. In the evening, I'd be so excited for my whole family to be home—we would play, hug, roll on the floor, go for a walk, and eat together as a unit. I would wait patiently to eat until my family was all accounted for, even if the plate was in front of me.

Pure nourishment for me was when everyone was together. This was my healing. That's the core value: everyone being together at dinner, connecting and talking about the day. This is what keeps the pack in check where we feel loved.

Lesson 10

PERSONAL POWER

Even though you may dress me up in funny outfits and take pictures of me, I know who I am, and I enjoy laughing with you. I don't take life too seriously because I want to be around for a long time. It is the seriousness we focus on in life that causes the pressure in our soul and dis-ease in our heart. We are here to have fun, experience this life, and be free. That is our personal power.

Humans mostly look at life situations, and quickly attach with expectation because of what one feels like he or she "needs" to do. When you're in your power, you can see beyond the circumstance of what is in front of you. Really, you're just being presented with an opportunity to learn and grow. To be truly empowered is to see that what is happening around us is only a limited view of what exists. What I learned in life is that *all* experiences help you move into your own power.

Teaching you to believe in yourself is my greatest gift. It is my goal to show you the way of simplicity, availability, and understanding. Feeling this on the inside allows life to happen without you getting sucked in or attached to what others do or think.

Believe in yourself always, without second guessing. Play like the puppy within. Be fully confident in your magnificence. We are all here to see this in one another and ourselves. I believe in you, and I know you believe in me

Lesson 11
HEALING

Healing happens when you are present and allow what you are feeling. Take the time to watch the birds, smell the flowers, lay in the sun, feel the ocean. These actions bring us in our body where we recognize our empowerment.

When I notice I am at the center of all things and breathe inward, I become the potential of my own natural state. Be here now and experience the flow of nature, the cosmos, and your own body rhythm, as it is who you truly are. Healing comes in many forms, and we have to be open to all the ways healing takes place in mind, body and spirit. Sometimes just feeling peace is the victory on the journey—this is our transformation without expectation. It is our energy and how we feel that takes precedence over this state, regardless of the outcome. Know you are made of energy, light, and vibration, first. You have the power to heal. What is locked within is reflected in your physical body. There is no looking back now. We are in this healing together. Watch and follow my lead.

Lesson 12
COMMUNICATION

The language of love is our truest form of communication. You feel it when I lay with you, when I look into your eyes for snacks, or when I sit in a perfect way so you know to take me out. This universal language lies under every spoken word, gesture, action, or bark. It permeates through all of us and extends the meaning of communication. It is the common denominator among all people and species. It is the same energy that allows us to feel nature, to feel the shift in our environment, to read body language, and to understand one's own gut intuition. This language of love bridges a soulful understanding and is a space between beings in which sacredness is held.

Many times we do this in silence without words—this is the ultimate form of communication. You practice with me, but it is something you can sense with everything and everyone. On this level, it allows us to see love, despite the differences in what we have learned or in language barriers. If you take the time and step into your vulnerability, it allows us to feel and sense more of the truth.

Remember, you can always communicate with me, even in the subtle silent moments. It may hold a different essence or require more of your attention to hear the message, but I am only a thought away. There are many forms of communication, but if you trust that there is a line that will never be broken, you will always have an open connection.

Lesson 13
KINDNESS

When other dogs cross my path, I don't judge them depending on the color of their fur, their size, life path, breed, or the choices they've made. I love first by wagging my tail; I am kind first by sniffing their butt. I may bark once or twice in protection when we first meet, but when it's over, it's over. We can play, be friends, and move on. If there were more of this in the world, and I don't mean butt sniffing, people would be in less pain and experience more joy.

The act of kindness starts when I see through each being as a part of who I am. I get to know them first, as I would want them to know me. In life, we all really want the same things —love, to be loved, and live in happiness. We just take different paths to get there sometimes. Honor that each person has had a journey that you are usually not aware of, and know it is being worked through. Be the support to help your fellow man, and see beyond the fear. Just be kind to one another, and make some love.

Here's a bark to Ellen:
"We need more kindness, more compassion, more joy, more laughter. I definitely want to contribute to that." - *Ellen Degeneres*

Lesson 14
JOY

I find Joy in all things. You could pet me, give me a treat, buy me my favorite singing toy, or take me on vacation. I show Joy by wagging my tail, hopping on the couch, or doing my puppy dance around the room. I never judge the act; it is all life, and life is to be celebrated. Even when you go away, I may be sad that I am not with you, but I am still joyful. Today celebrate your life and the life of your beloved companions.

Joy is a formula for living a celebrated life. A celebrated life means all experiences are acknowledged as something that is happening for You, not against you. This creates a mindset of abundance, moving you from being the victim of your circumstance to the creator of your life. When Joy is the foundation, you can allow the building blocks of who you are to be secured. Even when you experience sadness or anger, love or happiness—it's all energy. The emotion is the response, but when you choose to focus on Joy, you live in the appreciation of what it means to be alive, to be the spark in your own life. You have a choice! Focus on Joy and emit a quality of love. What do you choose to fill yourself with? How do you celebrate?

Most humans go through life forgetting to celebrate daily and acknowledging success both big and small. It is easy to be in Joy in the happy times. But even in sadness, you can still be in Joy by merely knowing that you can move forward Go deeper into who you are, and see all things as a test of your power. Joy is the appreciation of life. It helps you gain perspective and allows gratitude in every experience. Be the spark with no regrets, accept life, live full of joy.

Lesson 15
Gratitude

Allow me to be your reminder of gratitude. With every look, I am communicating gratitude for my life with you. We make each other shine. It is a moment-to-moment expression. Every time you think of me, use it as a sticky note to be grateful for all that you are. Collectively, if we really took the time to acknowledge all we have, not wanting something else or something different, we could exude presence and attract so much more good—good treats, good fun, tender love, and beach front dog houses.

The feeling of being satisfied with what Is, and knowing you are worth all the stars in the sky, opens up space for more of anything you desire. You have to be willing to give but also to receive nature's gifts. This balance is a message to the universe that you are grateful for every opportunity and that you are ready to receive even more.

Think about what is most important to you in life. Take a moment and bring it into your heart. What does it feel like? What would your life be like without it? The moment before protective thoughts come in reveals the infinite depth of gratitude—see it in all things, become aware. It is there for you to Be the magic in all that life holds.

Sometimes we are scared to feel deeply, and we push away gratitude. In being grateful, you recognize how it feels to open your heart and be vulnerable. When you live a life of gratitude you will not miss a beat, and you will know that you made every breath count. Many more things will show up in support of you in your life experience. The truth is, even the things you fight will become a lesson in gratitude. Be brave, let it in, and allow it to transform you.

Lesson 16

AGING

You may look at my pictures and see a little grey on my snout and a couple pounds on my belly. Don't let that fool you, I am as witty and spunky as ever. Remember aging is all in the head. You have control over the quality in which you age. If you just let chance take its course and do nothing, you will incur the "aging" diagnosis. If you follow these lessons and practice them daily, your body will sustain life much better.

Your spirit within is the same energy you were born with, and it remains the same through the ages. The process of life awakens you more to this energy within, but energy never grows old or dies. It is the same now as it was the day you were born without all the drama, trauma, and, expectations covering the purity. The energy that drops in, the true you, allows one to experience this life with vitality. Connect with that perfection and know that energy is unlimited and cannot age. This keeps you young at heart. Focus here and take the journey from your head to your heart. Make this energy more free and active instead of living within the bars of the mind. Be your own advocate for your health, and know you have the unlimited power to heal. Live your desired state!

Lesson 17
WILLINGNESS

I did whatever it took to breathe, thrive, and be here in the moment. I never focused on the things that didn't matter in life. I focused on having as many quality days as possible with my family. That made me happy because I loved my life and would do anything for sweet kisses and a filet.

My doctors always told me I had a will to live. They said I was a miracle dog and had to be surviving on love. I was in congestive heart failure for many years, and seven months before my passing my heart valves had ruptured. Even after this, the doctor was amazed that my heart continued to pump with force. I stayed lively, happy, and healthy. It never made sense medically how it all was happening, but we all knew with willingness, care, healing, and love, all things are possible, even the seemingly impossible.

The body is a miracle. When you pay attention to it, you will notice all the ways in which it can support you. Using the power of healing within, your will can follow the ways of nature. You will feel strength and peace always, regardless of your situation. If you are breathing, there is hope and material to work with.

Lesson 18
MIRACLES

The true essence of life is seen through the ways of animals, their way of being and walking the path. It all comes from love, and that is a miracle. That's why you love me so much. I AM a doorway to this vision! Close your eyes, listen, and feel all the miracles that surround you at all times. You can live this way, just follow my lead.

What if you could see everything as a miracle? You'd know, feel and sense that all the events around you are permeated with God source essence. You'd see that all aspects big and small are miracles being created for you to grow and get what you came here for. On top of it all, you'd know that you are the ultimate creator in your own universe. The more you can see through the fabric and into the source, the more you come to know that you are the living, breathing miracle. Life would be so much more interesting to feel this power. You see the miracle in me because I show you love unconditionally. Take this into your life, see all things as you see me, and watch your world-view expand. Thoughts become things, and you can influence how many miracles you recognize. Just ask, and your life will show you your magnificence.

Lesson 19
TRUST

I always trusted that you would provide me with all I need. To go through life with someone like you, who always walked by my side, helped us find comfort in the world and within ourselves. You trusted me because you could rely on our connection, which is a sacred space. The gift was for you to find your own space within and carry it within your heart. I was just your point of reference.

Everything is happening for a reason on the outside, but the safety comes from anchoring within and feeling trust. It is not about looking on the outside and trusting in someone or something but about trusting yourself. As we part ways, know that you played a role in helping me move to my next stage. We have learned our lessons and opened our hearts just a little more.

Understand that life is life and death is death. It is a cycle, be in it fully, and know there is more going on than you can see. Relax and flow with it. Otherwise, you will not know happiness. Resisting the process creates much sadness; without death, we do not have life and the start of a new journey. It is a continuous cycle like we see in nature. Trust and you will see that it is all going to work out. We planned for this, and we are both prepared. Remember healing takes place in many forms.

Lesson 20
GRACE

In all moments, I honor you without fearing what will happen to me. I watch the way you take care of me and love me with all your heart. I also witness how much fear you go into with the thought of what life will be like without me. My hope is that through the process of our journey together, you will be able to stay in love unconditionally, without focusing on the fear of the loss.

Even though you are in love, if you let go of the attachment to it all, the grander version of the relationship is much more freeing. This is what unconditional love looks like. It leaves space for Grace. When you begin to honor love in a different way, Grace comes in the picture. It happens when you can be in front of me and hold a space that you simply give IN to. You are not giving up, my friend, you are seeing that love does not die. It is unconditional. This is a state where you begin to know peace. There is nothing to earn. It is just a way to Be.

You have watched me do this for you in all your trials. It is your turn to show me the same faith, to operate this way in hard moments, and to be this divine influence. That is the ultimate way to honor me. There are no regrets because you are fully present without the illusion of what loss means for your life. I saw you in the days and moments before I left this physical space, and I could feel your Grace and the shift you have made. Know it helped me move to where I needed to go, and for you, it did the same. All is well, my friend.

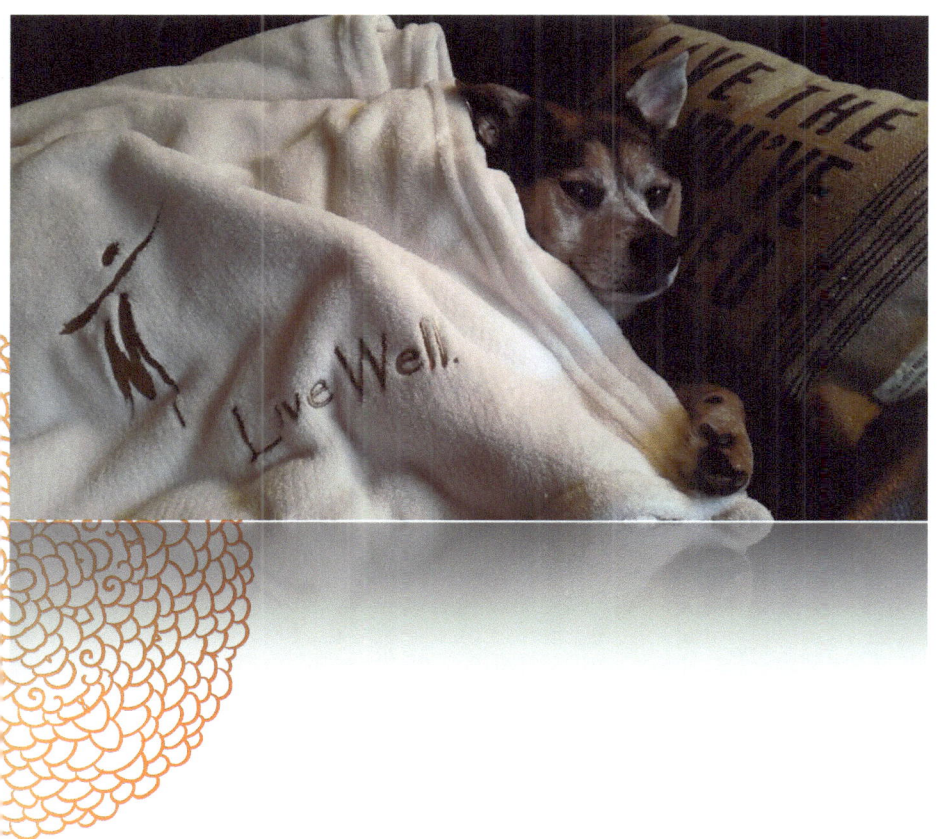

Lesson 21
SEE THE SIGNS

When I am gone, there will be moments when you miss my physical presence more than others. In that time, know you can ask for signs of me because I have not really gone anywhere. I am around you always. If you ask, you can feel my presence in different ways: you can see me as a magical sunrise or a brilliant rainbow. I am supporting you on your journey, and signs of love are everywhere—some very obvious and others, subtle reminders.

Want to connect with something you miss?
1. Ask for a sign
2. Be open to see the gifts
3. Feel the essence
4. Be in Gratitude

One day, I felt that my family was missing me… Jen and Jamie were asking me for a sign. I knew they both were open to seeing and feeling my presence. That morning, mirroring my Moms' tears, it was raining. Then, with some sun-rays, a rainbow reflected my love and support. I could see the disbelief in their faces. Is that Boo? They questioned…

I brought the rainbow closer to them, so they could feel the essence of me. They got the message, and I sensed their gratitude for this sign. What signs do you want to ask for? Ask and feel the essence.

Lesson 22
UNCONDITIONAL LOVE

I know your biggest fear is to lose me. This day has come. What I want you to know is your ultimate liberation is in what you fear. To meet the fear with Grace, moves you into the true knowing of unconditional love. It is said, the greater the love, the greater the fear, and you are feeling this. But, it is only here that you can begin to trust that I will never leave you. Feeling this will set you free.

It is time, and I have taught you well. Honor me and sense me in your day and in your dreams. You will feel a void, but the emptiness in anything is the space for a new beginning. Know that I support you always. Grieve for me, but also let me go, then it will be easier for you to sense me. I will be able to continue with my purpose, and you will with yours. Connect with my infinite energy, not just with the things of the past. I am a permanent imprint within you now, beyond the material. I am a new form, but I carry the memories of our love. The lessons will continue as I teach you the subtlety of energy and the truth beyond the veil.
Forever and always I will be your Captain, your Boo Boo.

VISIT DRJENFURCHT.COM

Learn more about Dr. Jen, her team, our programs and additional resources.

To book a prosperity strategy session use the link below and see how we can help you transform your health, wealth and happiness.

www.DrJenFurcht.com/session

THANKS FOR READING LIVE, LOVE, PAWS
Love, Dr. Jen, Dr. Jamie, and Team

www.ingramcontent.com/pod-product-compliance
Lightning Source LLC
Chambersburg PA
CBHW040057100426
42734CB00035B/80